# The Stranger's Compass

**By**

## David W. Thompson

# Table of Contents

# Acknowledgements

As always I thank God for the inspiration that flows from His Word. It gives me insight and a reason to write. The Scriptures guide and direct my steps everyday.

I thank my wife, Peggy for her love, support and encouragement. We have had a wonderful and blessed thirty-five year journey of marriage. I look forward to the next thirty-five.

To my Bible study group, many thanks for your fellowship and continued support. You are a great bunch of guys.

To Cathy and Brenda who check my work, there must be a special place in Heaven for women of such patience.

# Introduction

"Send forth your light and your truth, let them guide me; let them bring me to your holy mountain, to the place where you dwell."
Psalms 43:3 NIV

Welcome to my second offering of practical application of the Holy Scriptures. Life is not an easy journey. Those who try to navigate through it without God face an impossible task. If it is true as many say, "We only live to later die" then what purpose do we have for the journey? I am one who does not buy into the notion that life is an accident.

God has created this world and He is fully aware of what is happening in our lives. God wants to have a personal relationship with us. Part of that relationship is giving us the equipment we need to negotiate the twists and turns of our earthly life. God's Word is our source of direction as we travel toward the ultimate destination, eternal life in Heaven.

<u>The Stranger's Compass</u> is designed as a weekly Bible study for small groups. However, it can be used

as a daily devotional, also. It truly is practical application for many difficult questions or situations. My prayer is you will find light and truth in its pages.

David W. Thompson

# God's Compass

"Direct my footsteps according to your word;
let no sin rule over me." Psalm 119:133 NIV.

As we travel life's journey, we often seek direction on which path to take. God has given us a tool to help us make our way through the maze of this human life. His word is our compass. It points us to the right path. It can also rescue us when we, for whatever reason, have chosen the wrong route.

The Bible is God's Word. Just as a compass is designed to always point north, the Holy Scriptures point to God. God is our refuge and the final destination for all who believe. The problem is that the journey is long and often complicated by life situations. Sin is always ready to throw up a roadblock and confuse the traveler in order to misdirect the Christian's life.

All too often we get lost in this world of sin and lose sight of our destination. The best way to get back on the right path is to get into your Bible. The Bible is a most wonderful tool, but just like the compass, is useless unless it is used. What good is it to leave the compass in your backpack when you have become lost in the woods? Likewise, what good is the Bible if you do not open it up for answers when sin has you confused and lost in its grip?

More times than I want to admit, I have found myself in unfamiliar surroundings, tempted to take the wide highway that the world says is best. Without my moral compass, God's Word, it is far too easy to take the wrong road. Most of us, if we are truthful, will admit that at times we were foolish enough to choose a direction without reading the compass. And I do not know about anyone else, but, for me, that was not a smart move. I assure you that failing to consult your moral compass will lead you onto the path of regrets.

The traveler needs a compass. The more you read it and use it, the easier it is to stay on the path that God has planned for you. Read it often. Follow it always. It will lead you to God.

# Eating With the Pigs

"He longed to fill his stomach with the pods
that the pigs were eating, but no one gave him
anything." Luke 15: 16 NIV.

If you are familiar with the Bible, you will recognize this verse from the parable of the lost son.
In this story the son finally comes to his senses and
repents. The question that I have about this story is
how long will a person eat with the pigs?

First, we need to understand what eating with the
pigs really means. For the Jewish people the pig is
an unclean animal that is forbidden to eat. To even
be around such an animal was a major concern. So
the idea of actually eating the food set aside for them
was virtually unthinkable. For us, knowing that we
are not living in accordance to God's will in an area
of our life and not repenting of that action, has us fine
dining in the pig pen of sin.

If you have ever been around a hog farm, you
know that hogs will eat just about anything, even
their own offspring. When we are out of God's will,

we are no better. We will let our sin devour all the good things God has given us. Sin destroys our marriage through adultery, abuse and neglect. Sin eats our families and our friends. It destroys lives, businesses and churches, but we still continue in it. Why do we do this?

We are creatures who by our very nature are sinful. Sin entered the world through Adam and has been thriving ever since. Salvation through Jesus Christ has given us a new nature, but the old man does not die easily. The apostle Paul wrote, "So I find this law at work: When I want to do good, evil is right there with me." Romans 7: 21. Paul is telling us we have a choice. Sin is a choice we make. It is no one else's decision. To continue in sin is saying to God, "I like eating with the pigs". Maybe it is time to change our eating habits.

# Demons

"A man in the crowd called out, 'Teacher, I beg you to look at my son, for he is my only child. A spirit seizes him and he suddenly screams; it throws him into convulsions so that he foams at the mouth. It scarcely ever leaves him and is destroying him.'" Luke 9: 38-39 NIV

Make no mistake about it - I believe in demons. The Bible speaks of them, and I believe the Word of God. I do not claim to be an expert on such things. Quite frankly, I do not care to be.

I do not agree with the Hollywood version of demonic activity. I see nothing glorious or appealing in their depiction. Nevertheless, they are real. Some of the evil we face in this life can only be demonic in origin.

I also believe that we battle with personal demons. Very few families have not been touched by the demons of alcoholism, drug abuse, child abuse or sexual perversions. Parents, even good parents fight spiritual battles for the souls of their children. The once lovable child falls into the trap set by these demonic forces and suddenly finds that he or she is no longer in control of his physical body or mental faculties. The parents take action to protect the child, but find they are dealing with an ugliness that is hard, if not impossible, to describe.

How many times do we hear some person say, "That is not the person I know"? You can be sure that it is not the person you know. He has been invaded and is now being controlled by a force that he is unable to control. The parents will soon find that they too have no control over this demon.

However, there is hope. There is more to the story told in the Scriptures. The disciples were unable to drive out the demon. But Jesus Christ called for the boy. He rebuked the demon and healed the man's son and gave him back to him.

I believe in demons. But I have hope. Jesus is my hope.

# Anchors Aweigh

"Fearing that we would be dashed against the rocks, they dropped four anchors from the stern and prayed for daylight." Acts 27:29 NIV

The ship that was carrying the Apostle Paul was about to run aground on a rocky shore line. In an effort to hold off disaster, the sailors elected to drop anchors in the hope that the ship would then ride out the storm. God's grace was on Paul and the others on board.

The Bible tells us that there was no loss of life.

I was in a conversation with a friend and we were talking about the many trials that we face in life. I suddenly found myself saying something that turned out to be profound. "When you are the anchor in the storms of life, you will almost always be under water."

An anchor is of no use unless it is used. In the case of ships, the anchor is cast into the water in hopes of slowing or stopping the ship from running into trouble.

If you are a Christian spouse or parent, you are an anchor for your family. In times of trouble you will be called upon to keep the family from shipwreck. You must cast yourself into the seas of trouble. All the wisdom of this world is nothing more than a sandy bottom. The anchor cannot grab onto it and at best, will only slow the inevitable disaster.

However, the anchor that is cast on the rocks will find a way to hold fast and protect the family. In life there is only one rock that will hold your anchor fast. Jesus Christ is that rock. He is solid and unchanging. If you have anchored to him, He will hold you. The storms may come against you but they will not defeat you. He is our salvation. Nothing else will do.

As the anchor you will certainly feel the strain. There will be times when you feel that you will be pulled apart. You may fear that you will not hold on. Friend, remember this if nothing else. You are not holding on to Him. He is holding on to you. He holds you in the palm of His hand. There is not a storm that can tear you away from the Rock of Ages.

# I Hate Waiting

"Wait for the Lord; be strong and take heart
and wait for the Lord." Psalms 27:14 NIV

I cannot think of anyone who enjoys waiting.
Personally, I hate to wait. There may be a few
exceptions but not many. I wait with anticipation for
that tug on my fishing line. I calmly take in majesty
of God's creation as I sit in the woods waiting for the
opportunity to catch that trophy deer in my gun sites.
But these involve times that bring pleasure or joyous
excitement.

When I face times of opposition, persecution or
other trials I find myself anything but patient. Many
times I cry out, "Lord why does it take so long?".
When we hurt or someone we love is hurting, time
becomes a very big issue. My guess is it is because
very few of us enjoy pain or suffering.

At the time of this article, my family is being
bombarded on what seems to be all sides. The attack
is strong and in some cases very vicious. Yesterday,
I lost a beloved uncle to cancer. I have children with

serious health issues and marriage problems. My wife and I find ourselves in constant concern over the health and wellbeing of our parents. I could go on, but I think you get the point.

I want answers to my prayers, and I know that God will be faithful to answer them. The problem is I do not know when. I hate waiting when I am hurting. If most of the world is like me, it is no wonder that we are such a mess. The thought comes to me. If I hurt so much for others, what must my Heavenly Father feel about his children? He knows and feels my pain and sorrow. He cares about my hurt. He even cares about my lack of patience and reluctance to wait. God does not want to harm me. But he does want to grow me and use me for His glory.

I resolve to wait for the Lord because I know He is faithful. I will see the answers to my prayers in this life or the next when I stand in His presence. Sometimes you just have to wait. The problem is I do not like to wait.

# Losing Your Life

"Whoever finds his life will lose it, and
whoever loses his life for my sake will find
it." Matthew 10:39 NIV

My wife and I were having a discussion the other
day. The topic was on how we have been able
to remain happy and content in our marriage through
the many hardships over the last thirty four years.

First and foremost, we credit God and His
marvelous grace. Two people in a marriage relationship without God stand alone to face the cruelties of
life. With God at your side you are never alone. If I
am going to go through trials and tribulations here
on this earth, it only makes sense to stand close to
the Creator of the heavens and the earth. The apostle
Paul tells us that "His grace is sufficient".

Beyond God's grace there is something that we
have learned. If we want a life or marriage that is
blessed and truly fulfilling, we must lose our own
life. We must give up our selfish ambitions. My life
cannot be about me.

I have watched others struggle and I have struggled myself with self-centeredness. When it is about me, others suffer. When I make the decision to lay my life down in my marriage, I become more concerned about the needs of my spouse. I find myself looking for ways to make her feel better about herself. A wife with good self-esteem is a treasure indeed. Come on guys. Think about it. There is some truth to the saying, "When momma is not happy, nobody is happy."

A happy marriage is a giving marriage. I find the more that I give of myself, the more that I receive in my relationship. Think about the verse for today. If I lose my life in serving God, I actually find it. Then why wouldn't the same principle apply to my marriage? Self gets in the way of our relationship with God. Self will also hurt the relationship you have with your spouse. The perfect relationship is built on selfless devotion.

# The Sacrifice of Praise

"Through Jesus, therefore, let us continually offer to God a sacrifice of praise, that is, the fruit of the lips that confess his name."
Hebrews 13:15 NIV

How can praise be a sacrifice? This is a very interesting question, one that may be best clarified by a series of questions.

Do you praise God when you are happy and things are going your way? How about when things have been turned upside down and the storms of life are buffeting you from all sides? Do you praise him in good health? Do you praise him when pain racks your body and just moving becomes a difficult task? Do you give praise in time of great gain, as well as in time of utter loss? Do you praise God even when you do not feel like it?

Can we agree that praising God when life is good is not a difficult feat? But praising God when life is hard and difficult to understand can truly become a sacrifice. When you or a family member is facing cancer, you may find it hard, if not impossible, to praise God. When a divorce is looming for a loved one, it is much easier to petition God than praise Him.

When we are at church and the congregation is singing songs of praise, there are times when the words cannot get past my lips. I want to be able to praise Him at all times and at all cost. But want and doing are not the same.

The issue for me, and I am sure, many others, is focus. Where do I focus my attention? Is it on me and my problems or the one who is greater than me and any problem that I might face?

Lord help me to sacrifice myself. Help me to give up and let you do what you desire with my life. You gave the ultimate sacrifice at Calvary. That one act deserves my eternal praise and adoration. I praise the name of Jesus Christ, my Redeemer and closest friend. Amen.

# Take Him at His Word

"Jesus replied, 'You may go. Your son will live.' The man took Jesus at his word and departed." John 4:50 NIV

How well do we fare at taking God at his word? Is it easier when all is well? Or do we even give it a thought? How about when times are tough? Are we willing to take God's promises and hold fast to them? Do the tough trials make us throw up our hands and declare, "I don't believe God will help me"?

It really boils down to belief and trust. If I read or hear the Word of God, yet I do not act on it as truth, I either do not believe it or do not trust it. Or maybe it is both. No matter which scenario it may be, it is not a good one.

God's Word is either true or it is not. We do not have the luxury of picking and choosing from the Bible what we want to call truth. It is either all true or it is all a lie. If I call God a liar, then I am lost in my sin. I will be the first to admit that knowing the truth and living it is not always easy or comfortable.

What I want to happen sometimes does not line up with what God says will happen. And we all know that what He says is what will happen.

If I choose contrary to the Word, even though I know it to be true, I am essentially saying I trust my own human judgment and understanding over God's. One word describes this kind of thinking - dumb. I have a wall plaque in my office. The saying on it goes like this, "You can educate ignorance but you can't fix stupid." I believe that God's Word is true and therefore, law. If I act contrary to the law, I am a lawbreaker. When that law is God's, I am a sinner.

So there you have it. If we say God's Word is not true, we are sinners because of our unbelief. If we know that the Word is true and we act in a manner contrary to it, we are sinners because we willingly break the law. This is not a good place to be. The solution is simple. Trust God and believe his Word.

# The Storms of Life

"He replied, 'You of little faith, why are you so afraid?' Then he got up and rebuked the winds and the waves, and it was completely calm." Matthew 8:26

Do you have some storms blowing in your life? Maybe not at this moment, but you can see the dark clouds gathering on the horizon. It is only a matter of time for all of us. Sooner or later the storms of life will rage against us.

Mankind does not have the ability to build a shelter secure and safe enough to withstand all the storms that come our way. Only one shelter can be found that will keep us safe. That one has been designed by the Creator of the heavens and the earth. No expense has been spared in its construction. In fact, God did not spare his own son, Jesus, when it came to building our safe haven. It is available to all who place their faith and trust in Jesus Christ.

So here is the big question. Knowing that God has provided shelter in the storms, why do we have so much fear and lack of faith when those storms hit? It seems to me that we grab on to the first hope or fix that we see. Usually, these are man-made and offer little to no true protection for us. They are only quick or temporary solutions that offer no lasting results. Why just survive when we can truly be safe?

I have noticed over many years that storms come to test and to teach us. They test our faith, and we learn through the success we find by standing firm with God or failing by trusting in our own inventions. Sadly, I have been a slow learner.

But, I am tired of failing and dealing with the fear of uncertainty. I resolve to seek refuge in God from the storms that come my way. I will wait upon the Lord. He is my shelter and protector. The psalmist said, "He who dwells in the shelter of the Most High will rest in the shadow of the Almighty." Psalm 91:1.

# Still Going and Going

"You need to persevere so then when you have done the will of God, you will receive what he has promised." Hebrews 10:36 NIV

Please allow me to address my own pity party. I get so tired and discouraged these days.

Life hits with a full head of steam. One crisis follows another and another with what appears to be no interruption. I cry out to God for help and answers. The answer comes in a quiet voice saying, "Wait, be patient, keep going." Not exactly what I am looking for.

So here I am, decision time again. Do I trust God or not? Do I stay in the Word or do I try something else? Will I give up or stand fast? Hey, why does it have to be so black and white? Give me options, lots of options! Is this it? Yes, this is it. I either trust God or I don't.

Well, the second choice is not really an option for me. His Holy Spirit resides in me. I know it because I feel his presence. He guides me daily through my hurt, pain and suffering. He attends to my broken heart. He lights the path in front of me so that I do not fall. He transforms the lives of people I know and love. How can I not trust Him?

So, there you have it. It is time to once again stop my whining, hold my head up and put one foot in front of the other and accomplish the tasks that God has set in front of me today. One breath, one step, one specific moment in time to serve the Master. It may hurt. It may be unpleasant. But, I have to keep going. I must persevere. The reward may not be in this lifetime, but I know that there is a reward waiting for me in Heaven.

Therefore, I will keep going and going until God decides that I have done enough.

# Mountains

"Jesus replied, 'I tell you the truth, if you have faith and do not doubt, not only can you do what was done to the fig tree, but also you can say to this mountain, "Go, throw your self in the sea," and it will be done. If you believe, you will receive whatever you ask for in prayer.'" Matthew 21:21-22 NIV

Jesus had just demonstrated his power over nature by making a fig tree wither that did not bear fruit. He used this opportunity to encourage and challenge his disciples in their faith. We too can learn much from this passage. God is concerned in all areas of our lives. Small or large, it does not matter; He wants us to find strength and victory in all things.

It is easy for me to feel strong and victorious when I am able, with God's help, to overcome a small trial. But when a big one comes my way, it is much easier to whine and whimper. I can all too quickly run up the flag of surrender and let the mountain of a problem defeat me. I know this is not how I should be, but I am never as good or strong as I imagine myself to be.

There are times when I stand in my faith and offer my prayers to God, and He delivers just like He promised to do. So why do I sometimes let the mountain intimidate me? My humanness tells me that when a mountain is in the way you can go around it, over it, through it, or you can stop and turn around. God's Word tells me there is another option.

Why not just move the mountain? Is that possible? Well, of course it is.

Let's go back to a picture of nature. If you watch the news, sooner or later you will see a story about an earthquake. Whole mountains are leveled. One minute it is there and then it is gone, flattened in the blink of an eye. If it can happen in nature, how can I not believe that God, who created all nature, isn't ready, willing and able to remove my personal mountains? God is capable. The problem is my unwillingness to ask for help. Sounds like pride or a lack of faith, doesn't it? Either case is not good.

So what am I going to do? From now on every mountain will be met with prayer and faith. I will petition God, believe his Word and wait for him to clear the way.

# Too Busy

"But Martha was distracted by all the preparations that had to be made. She came to him
and asked, 'Lord, don't you care that my sister
has left me to do the work by myself? Tell
her to help me!' 'Martha, Martha,' the Lord
answered, 'you are worried and upset about
many things, but only one thing is needed.
Mary has chosen what is better, and it will
not be taken from her.'" Luke 10:40-42 NIV

Can a Christian be too busy serving others? Yes,
I think so. Serving others in the name of Christ
is a vital part of our earthly mission. Martha obviously had a servant's heart, and I do not criticize her
for that. The issue I get from this passage is we need
to be careful that we do not become so consumed
with service that we miss out on the real blessing of
spending time with our God.

I remember from my childhood that my mother
and father often invited pastors and evangelists into
our home for dinner. Someone special was coming

to our house on Sunday, and my mother would go into overdrive. The house had to be clean and tidy, not an easy task when you have three young sons. She would set out the good dishes and they would be placed on the dining room table. We only used this table on special occasions.

The kitchen was alive with clamor. I can still smell the roast cooking. The guest would arrive and father would entertain him until dinner was on the table. I do not have time to fully describe dinner to you, but one thing I can assure you of, with my two brothers and me at the table, it was often entertaining and eventful. If something was not spilt, dropped or broken, it was a true miracle.

Dinner was over in no time. Father and our special guest would move to the living room and begin conversing on all sorts of subjects. I am sure some of them were spiritual in nature. I am not absolutely certain about the conversations because we, the boys, usually were already heading outside to play. We called it play. My parents called it, "Thank God they are outside."

Mother, in the meantime, was cleaning off the table, washing dishes and wondering when she would find time to do the normal daily chores before her boys would come back in and need something. In the end, Mother would be able to grab only a few minutes of prime time with our guest.

How much time are you leaving for Jesus? Are you so busy serving that you can't find time to talk with God? Slow down today and take some time to get to know your most special guest.

# No, I Don't Understand

"BUT MARK this: There will be terrible times in the last days." 2 Timothy 3:1 NIV

This has been a week of tragedy for our country. A student for reasons unknown at this time went on a killing rampage at Virginia Tech University. The loss of life and talent is staggering. Our nation is stunned. Everyone is asking the same questions. Why and how could this happen?

I would like to say I know the answer, but I don't. I would like to tell you that it will never happen again, but I can't. I wish I could assure everyone that they are safe from such evil actions, but it would not be true.

If you continue with this passage from the second book of Timothy, the apostle Paul gives us a list of adjectives that describe mankind's attitudes in the last days. "People will be lovers of themselves, lovers of money, boastful, proud, abusive, disobedient to their parents, ungrateful, unholy, without love, unforgiving, slanderous, without self-control, brutal, not lovers of good, treacherous, rash, conceited, lovers of pleasure rather than lovers of God" 2 Timothy 3:2-4. I wonder how many of these will apply to the killer by the time the investigation is completed?

I do know this. Good people often suffer. It will be interesting to see how those who have been personally affected and who know Christ as their Lord and Savior handle themselves in comparison to those who do not have a relationship with God. I would hope that they would fare better and be good examples to follow, but that may not be the case. All I can do at this time is to pray for all those who have been touched by this terrible act and ask that God will carry them through this time of loss and grief. I can also watch those around me. If they seem to be depressed or disturbed about what has happened, I can be there to give comfort and counsel.

Why did this happen? I just don't know. Could we be in the last days? It certainly looks that way. I do believe that God is in control and nothing that is done will go unpunished.

# Life is a Puzzle

"And he is not served by human hands, as if he needed, because he himself gives all men life and breath and everything else. From one man he made every nation of men, that they should inhabit the whole earth; and he determined the times set for them and the exact places where they should live." Acts 17:25-26 NIV

God has blessed us with grandchildren. At this time, we have six wonderful little people who love us unconditionally. The last two came as a set (twins) almost four years ago. One of their favorite play time projects is to put together puzzles. While participating in this particular form of entertainment I received a great lesson from one of them.

Alex loves to work on puzzles and his favorite part of the exercise is to put the last piece into place. It does not matter if there are ten or forty pieces; he makes sure that the last piece is always in his hand. He will always hold one piece back so that he can place the final piece of the puzzle in the picture. He already understands that the picture is not complete until the last piece is laid.

That is the way life works. Each day we live, every choice we make is a piece of our puzzle. Events both good and bad help to shape the pieces as we learn to cope, rejoice and mourn. Our mistakes and our victories are all part of our puzzle. Piece by piece we form our life story. Each trial we live through forms more of the picture. Every tear finds its place. Each moment we share with others fits into a given space.

Unlike the puzzles that we buy and put together, life does not have a precise picture to follow. The only one who knows what our life will ultimately look like is God. He has given us instructions for life in His Word. He also has given us a glimpse of what life can and should be by sending His Son and showing us by example how to live for God. Our Heavenly Father has generously given to His children the Holy Spirit to guide us in placing the pieces of our life in the correct places.

In the end, it is God, who holds the last piece of our puzzle in His sovereign hand. Only He knows when our earthly puzzle is going to be completed. Until He places the last piece in place we continue piecing together our life that is sometimes very puzzling.

# Are You Sinking?

But when he saw the wind, he was afraid and beginning to sink, cried out, "Lord, save me!" Immediately Jesus reached out his hand and caught him. "You of little faith," he said, "why did you doubt?" Matthew 14:30-31 NIV

I have been having that sinking feeling lately, and the Lord brought this passage to mind to assure me that He knows where I am. Trials and tribulations are like the waves on an angry sea. In our weakness we see them as insurmountable obstacles. In our doubt we allow ourselves to be overwhelmed by what we see and feel.

I find it interesting that the Scriptures said that "he saw the wind". The truth is he saw and felt the effects of the wind but not the actual wind, which is, of course, invisible. Many of the things that get us down are just the visible effects of the deeper invisible spiritual battles that are waged around us.

I take comfort in the fact that when Peter cried out to the Lord there was an immediate reaction. Jesus reached out his hand and caught him. I believe that when times get tough or dangerous, I need to cry out to God. Only He is able to catch me when doubt and fear have caused me to begin to sink in my faith walk. I also realize that when I am forced to cry out for help due to my lack of faith, Jesus asks me the same question, "Why did you doubt?"

So, for today at least, I have resolved to keep my eyes focused on my Savior and the greater purposes of God's Kingdom and not on the trials that try to pull me down. I had rather try to walk on the water than wade or swim through the waves that come from the unseen spiritual battles. May the Lord keep all of us from doubt. Amen

# A World Gone Neb

He said, "Is not this the great Babylon I have built as the royal residence, by my mighty power and for the glory of my majesty?"
Daniel 4:30 NIV

We seem to live in a world that is very much full of itself. I hate to pick on Hollywood celebrities, but they are such an easy target, so I will. You cannot turn on the news without seeing that someone famous has taken a fall. His life has been so about me and what I have done that he often appears to be acting in an insane manner. Is it possible that he is suffering from the same insanity that fell upon Nebuchadnezzar, King of Babylon?

Like some of today's stars, he thought he had everything - position, power and wealth. He had so much that he failed to see that all blessings come from God. God is the source of all true blessings. In his pride Nebuchadnezzar claimed that everything good and wonderful had been created by his own hand. This pride became the source of his insanity.

He spent a long period of time isolated from people and become a man with the appearance of a wild animal. The Bible tells us he ate grass with the cattle. Now I consider that pretty crazy.

I wish that I could say that this type of "me" attitude is only found in Hollywood. Unfortunately, it can be found everywhere. It is in politics, business, schools, families and yes, even in our churches. Don't you know someone who acts as if the world revolves around him, someone who can become angry over the slightest decision made without his approval? Do you have a boss who cannot let anybody else make a decision? Maybe you know someone who wants special favors because of who he is. Have you ever known someone who took the credit for something that another person had done?

If you don't know someone who matches one of the descriptions above, you are not a citizen of this planet. The simple truth is the world needs to wake up and understand it is not about us and what we want or do, but all about God and what brings Him glory and praise. We need to be careful so that we do not end up eating grass with the cattle. Personally, I would rather eat the cattle.

# My Belief Makes Me Who I Am

Then the man said, "Lord, I believe," and he worshiped him. John 9:38 NIV

This morning I received an e-mail from an old and dear friend. He attached a survey that would grade the potential candidates for the presidency according to how I answered several questions concerning moral and social issues. When it was completed, I found that I was much more aligned to one political party than the other. This did not come as a great shock to me.

We are the product of what we truly believe. The true nature of a man is found in his heart, not in his words or ideas. What we hold dear is evident in our actions. We call our beliefs many things. Those that are changeable we call knowledge because true facts or evidence can change those beliefs. Others we call convictions because they are matters that affect our inner being. They are unchanging in nature.

Convictions are not swayed by popular thought. They are the foundation of who we are.

My belief that Jesus Christ is my Lord and Savior is the cornerstone of my foundation. He is the beginning and the end of whom and what I am. All my other beliefs either work in unity or in contradiction to this one central truth. Those that do not work in unity are those that are subject to change, and they do change as God reveals the facts to me through the Holy Spirit. What I thought to be true suddenly is changed by God's truth, and a conviction is formed, and I become more defined. The more defined I become the more clearly I know who I am.

Interestingly enough, the more I understand who I am the more the world will see who I truly am. I hope the people that I come in contact with will see me for my true beliefs because they should dictate my actions. I realize that may not always be the case since I have need for more defining in my life. But, hopefully, the next time you see me and we have time to talk, you will catch at least a glimpse of the one I worship, Jesus Christ.

# What Was I Thinking?

"But the plans of the Lord stand firm forever, the purposes of his heart through all genera-tions." Psalms 33:11 NIV

Have you ever asked yourself this question? If you are an adult and have not been living in a vacuum, the answer certainly must be yes. Recently I have been asking this question on a frequent basis.

I remember as a young husband I had plans and ideals for my family. You know - things like two people meet, start a relationship, fall in love, marry, have children, the children later continue the cycle and everyone is happy, right? What was I thinking? Maybe I watched too much "Leave it to Beaver" and "The Waltons" for my own good. Life, no matter how good you plan it is always ready to sneak up behind you and take a bite out of your tail.

How many times have you taken great care to plan a vacation only to have it interrupted or even canceled at the last moment due to an outside force such as work, family or a tragedy? Can you count them? Someone once said, "Plans are subject to change." I just did not realize that they meant every single one I make. Ok, maybe I am overreacting. But, aren't there days when it sure seems that way?

I thank God, that one plan went exactly as scheduled. It was not my plan, but it did involve you and me. God loved us so much that long before we were born a plan was made to save us from our sin and the punishment that the Law demanded. Our Heavenly Father's plan to send his one and only Son to be our sacrifice was perfect in every way. Satan and all his demons could not alter the plan. In fact, they were part of God's plan to bring salvation to mankind. Never once did God say, "oops" or "that did not go like I thought".

Friend, let me assure you that while the plans of man can be flawed, the plans of God are and will always be perfect. I think that should give us all great comfort.

# A Snake on the Path

"In the paths of the wicked lie thorns and snares, but he who guards his soul stays far from them." Proverbs 22:5 NIV

Recently, my wife and I were hiking on a nature trail. What started as a boardwalk pathway, able to accommodate two people side by side, ultimately turned into a dirt path winding through a marsh. My wife suggested that I take the lead in our little expedition, and in her words, "be her protector from any wild creatures that might be out there." I gladly took the lead position (After all I am the man) and headed forward into the marsh. After a few minutes, the beauty and uniqueness of this natural setting began to capture my attention.

About halfway through our two-mile trek, my wife gave a very loud shout of alarm. "There's a snake on the path!" I turned around startled. My wife stood on the extreme edge of the dirt path pointing to a long black object. I immediately went to her and looked at the source of her concern. Sure enough, it was a black snake about four feet in length. I had obviously stepped right over it without noticing. I assured her that she had nothing to fear, that the snake was more afraid of her than she was of it. I admit that was probably a poor choice of words. She was not at all comforted by my words. I was supposed to protect her, and I had failed in my duty.

Life can be very much like that day on the path. You get so busy with your surroundings or daily routine that you step right over temptation and miss it completely. You might think it is a good thing to miss temptation. But what if that snake had been poisonous? I could have placed my wife and myself in great danger.

We are called to guard ourselves and our families from Satan's efforts to tempt us. While life may be beautiful and distracting, we can not afford a lack of vigilance. The old serpent may be lying in the middle of our path waiting to take a bite out of us. He desires to pull us from the path of righteousness and will do exactly that if we do not pay attention. My friends, let us enjoy life, but may we keep our eyes on where we are going.

# Looking for the Lighthouse

"For this is what the Lord has commanded us: 'I have made you a light for the Gentiles, that you may bring salvation to the ends of the earth.'" Acts 13:47 NIV

My wife and I just returned from a vacation on the East coast. We traveled much of the New Jersey coastline in search of lighthouses. You would not think that finding a lighthouse would be a difficult task. Well, think again.

With map in hand we set out to visit some historical sites along the route. Every so often along the road we traveled, the map would indicate that a historic lighthouse was nearby. We would diligently follow the directions and the occasional road sign in an effort to locate the lighthouse. How anyone can hide a thing as large as a lighthouse is beyond me. But try as we might, we either ran out of road or out of hope before we could find our elusive targets. I say targets because, if you can believe it, we tried three different lighthouses, and we were unable to find any of them.

My wife gave up on ever being able to see a real coastal lighthouse. As we pondered whether the state of New Jersey really wanted people to see these historic sites or if they truly existed, there it was. No, not a lighthouse, but a sign indicating that yet another one could be found just a little further down the coast. Well, being from Missouri and also being somewhat stubborn, I determined to give it one more shot. My wife agreed to the plan, but I could tell she had little hope that we would succeed.

We followed the map. We followed the signs. We drove and drove, but no lighthouse. After some time we were out of road and we had not seen a sign in the last ten minutes. Then I heard the question, "Are you going to give up?" My answer was, "No, absolutely not." Then the next question, "Are you sure?" I gave my answer, "We are going to find that lighthouse." Suddenly, I saw it ahead. No, not the lighthouse, but another sign for it. We drove another quarter of a mile and the road made a sharp left and wouldn't you know it, a lighthouse. It had been hidden by houses and trees. We had been so close, yet unable to see it.

What keeps people from finding God's lighthouse? What gets in the way? He has given a map. It is called the Bible. Jesus fulfilled hundreds of prophesies to give all the signs that people could ever want. Yet, some people can not find the Light. Is there really too much in the way? Maybe, people need a guide. That is where you and I come in. We must let the light of Jesus Christ shine through us and become a lighthouse for God.

# Respect

"Make it your ambition to lead a quiet life, to mind your own business and to work with your hands, just as we told you, so that your daily life may win the respect of outsiders and so that you will not be dependent on anybody." 1 Thessalonians 4:11-12 NIV

I am reminded of a birthday party for my nephew that occurred several years ago. It was his thirteenth birthday and all the family had gathered together to celebrate. He seemed rather dismal during the party and someone finally asked him what was bothering him. His reply has stuck in the back regions of my mind and occasionally some situation brings it back to full bloom. He said, "I thought that when I got up this morning that people would treat me different, but now I see that being older did not make any difference."

What a shock to his ego that realization must have been. I can understand the poor boy's confusion. The world wants us to believe that respect is something that should be automatic. The verse above tells me that respect must be won or earned. My nephew had placed his hope for respect in age. While age can play a part in gaining respect, it is not the only criteria for earning it.

Today, some people believe that respect is due them from their wealth, fame, intellect, physical appearance or some other "superior worldly characteristic." If respect comes from living a quiet life, how many of us have been disqualified from earning someone's respect? If minding your own business is a quality that earns respect, how many other opportunities have been lost? If hard work is required to gain respect, has our laziness cost us?

The Bible is clear. We are to give respect, and I believe that is a part of earning it. But do not be deceived. Respect is not a given. If I am honored just because I have wealth, am I truly being respected? If I receive praise because I can run faster or jump higher than others, does that make me respectable? I think not. There are some very great athletes in our prison system. You will find some who are or were very wealthy behind those same prison bars. Age may give you gray hair, but it is not a free ride to respect.

The respect we need to seek comes from our Christ-like characteristics. Jesus was not flashy or obnoxious. He was not afraid to work, and he was never accused of being a gossip. I hope to be content with winning respect of men by emulating my Savior.

# A Job Story

"After Job had prayed for his friends, the Lord made him prosperous again and gave him twice as much as he had before." Job 42:10 NIV

I know a young lady who has had a time of testing just like Job. In fact, I know her very well. She is my daughter. She was living the ideal life for her as a wife, mother and homemaker. She had married her childhood sweetheart. They had two great boys. They had purchased a home and all was well.

One day she was given the news that she had a rare and incurable kidney disease. She was told that ultimately she would need to have a transplant to survive. Her marriage had been showing signs of stress for some time, but then things began to escalate. She found out that her husband had been unfaithful to her. She lost a baby girl when she miscarried early in a pregnancy. After the miscarriage she was told by her doctor that she would never be able to have any more children. Other problems were uncovered and ultimately the marriage was lost. Financial circumstances forced her to sell her home and move 700 miles to live with her parents. All she owned was put into a U-Haul trailer and a couple of cars and transported to Missouri.

My daughter, her two sons, and two dogs lived with us for almost two years. She dealt with depression and disappointment. She had to live with the fact that her now ex-husband was not willing to send support for his children. Jobs came and jobs were lost. Amazingly, she never gave up on God.

Now, let me give you the good news. God has done miraculous things in her life. First, He has healed one of her kidneys completely and is slowly restoring the other. Secondly, a new man was brought into her life. They are now married and he is a fine Christian man who would make any father-in-law proud. They have their own home in the country with plenty of room for children and dogs. She has two wonderful stepsons that are true treasures. And finally, she has just given us a new granddaughter. Yes, God has restored her womb and given her a little girl to replace the one that was lost.

God has restored to her everything she had lost and then some. We wait to see what else may be coming to her because God gave back double to Job. For those who think the story of Job is just a fictional creation I say, "Think again." What a mighty God we serve!

# Patience in the Battle

"Be joyful in hope, patient in affliction and faithful in prayer." Romans 12:12 NIV

Once again God is teaching me a lesson. This lesson is particularly frustrating since it involves my writing. As I write this lesson my first book has just come off the presses.

The book took a year to write and nearly another year to get it published. The publishing process was anything but easy. I guess I should not have been surprised that obstacle after obstacle lined the way.

First, I took the advice of someone and put the book on what is called a flash drive. They told me that it would be resistant to corruption, and I need not worry about saving the material on my personal computer. I am sure that you can guess what happened next. Yes, the flash drive somehow got corrupted and the entire text was lost. We were able to go into my personal computer and salvage the material, but all the corrections that I had made on the flash drive were lost. Even though I had made hard copies and had hoped to be able to scan them and make them usable, that did not work either.

My publisher tried to use the scanned documents, but in the end it just would not work. The next step was to take the uncorrected documents and make all the corrections over again. I spent eight hours comparing the hard copies and the recaptured computer documents. I was sure I had caught most, if not all, the errors. I was wrong. After the publisher sent me a copy to review, I was able to find more errors. I sent in the corrections and reviewed each one when the corrected text was sent back to me. I was finally able to say, "Go to press."

A few weeks passed and my book appeared on my doorstep. I cannot explain how excited I was. The book looked wonderful. I must admit that a sense of pride rose in my chest, and I was truly thankful that God had allowed me to write a book. I knew I had rushed things, but I was certain that while it may not be perfect, it was certainly good enough. Wrong again, David. My wife found some errors. Then she found some more.

Didn't someone say, "Pride goes before the fall?"

After a brief discussion with my wife and the publisher, we decided to stop the printing of the book. I now have a retired English teacher reviewing and correcting the entire text. It will not go to press unless everyone is satisfied. Writing my first book and getting it published has been nothing short of a wild and crazy journey, and it appears not to be over. Oh, by the way, the name of the book, <u>A Stanger's Journey</u>. Go figure.

# Pain on My Brother's Face

"Finally, all of you, live in harmony with one another; be sympathetic, love as brothers, be compassionate and humble." 1 Peter 3:8 NIV

Once in a while we have the opportunity to give comfort and show compassion for a brother. For me the problem has always been knowing when and where to make myself available to those who are hurting. I have been accused of being uncaring or hard because I intentionally do not force my compassion on someone else. I do not know if it is because of fear that they may react negatively or if I just do not read their face or outward appearance well.

We have brothers and sisters in the faith who are hurting. Many are going through difficult trials that we may not be able to imagine. One of my employees has a spouse who is dealing with cancer. It is inoperable and ultimately terminal. He has had to balance work and care giving and has done an admirable job. I am close enough to the situation that I can easily recognize the pain and stress that he shows. If I did not have the personal knowledge that I do, I would not be able to see the pain. He handles himself in such a manner that the outside world might not ever know what he and his spouse are going through.

When I am aware of pain and suffering, I make myself available. By available, I mean that I let people know I am ready to help in any area that I can. I will not force myself upon them. Some people handle trials differently than others. Some are in need of comfort while others, with the aide of God, are able to and are more comfortable in making the painful journey alone. I do not know if my plan of action is the right one or not. One may let us know where he needs assistance and another may feel that it is an imposition and may never ask. I am certain though that at least offering is better than not noticing.

My goal, and one that I hope other Christians will take on, is to become better readers of pain on our brother's and sister's faces. In doing that, we can become more available to those who need and want our Godly compassion.

# Love like a Deep Snow

"Above all, love each other deeply, because love covers over a multitude of sins." 1 Peter 4:8 NIV

I woke up this morning and had extra work to do. Overnight, we had received about four inches of snow. I did not put on my normal work clothes, but dressed in warm, more labor-friendly apparel. My snow blower was in the corner of the garage ready to go, but first I had to move several bicycles belonging to my grandchildren. Fueled up and ready for action, I opened the garage door and felt the frigid air against my face. This was going to be fun.

We do not get a lot of snow in east central Missouri. My skills in blowing snow are not finely tuned. During the first pass, I made most of the snow went up in the air and then back into my face. If I was not fully awake before, I certainly was then. It did not take long to judge the direction of the wind and set a course that would be more comfortable for me. Fortunately, it was what I would call a dry snow and it was easy to remove. What normally would have taken an hour or better was finished in half the time. My wonderful wife had coffee ready when I came in the house and was full of compliments about the service I had rendered.

The snowfall was beautiful and nothing lying on the ground could be seen. I was reminded of the passage above. Love is like snow. The deeper the love, the more we will overlook the transgressions or character flaws of another. Married couples usually will find a way to work around certain issues that they might not be willing to do with the next door neighbor. Parents may be more gracious to their own children than their children's friends. Most of us are more forgiving of family and close friends than we are of people we do not know. A deeper love seems to be the key.

So, I pose this question. How deep is your love? The answer is found in how much you are willing to forgive. Fortunately for us, the love that God has for His children is deeper than we can possibly imagine. It is so deep that once He has forgiven a sin, it is forever forgotten by Him. Imagine our life if we would do the same. Let it snow. Let it snow. Let it snow.

# Integrity

"The integrity of the upright guides them, but the unfaithful are destroyed by their duplicity." Proverbs 11:3 NIV

I guess it should come as no surprise that this world does not place much value on integrity. Here is a case in point. A few years ago one of my customers wanted to sell his car dealership. He began negotiations with another dealer who wanted to expand his territory. A price was set and preparations were made to close the deal. During this time our institution received an anonymous phone call reporting that our dealer was selling cars out of trust. Knowing our customer well, we did not get excited, but we did go out and make an inspection, which proved that the phone call was false. After the dealership was sold, the buyer admitted that he had placed the phone call in an attempt to force the price down. Would you want to buy a car from this sort of person? I have not referred a single customer to the dealer since he made his actions known. Where has integrity gone?

Unfortunately, this kind of behavior sometimes can be found in our churches. When people take issue with another, they often begin to talk to others and make statements that mislead or are, in fact, outright lies. I remember a pastor friend of mine who was accused of "misappropriating church funds". The person making the accusations gathered his support through the avenue of gossip. The pastor's character was questioned, and he ultimately left the church. An audit was ordered and he was proven innocent. In fact, it was proven that he had absolutely no access to the church funds. The damage was done, and the church was split and is still healing from the event. The pastor moved on to greener pastures and the accuser went to another church.

I am not saying that all churches suffer from a lack of integrity. But, if even one does, that is too many. When we, the church, display the same worldly values of the non-believing world, we lose credibility. We are destroying ourselves and our witness. Integrity lost can never be restored. Stay upright and let integrity lead you. The way that seems right to the world is more-than-likely wrong.

# Frustration and Worry

"Who of you by worrying can add a single hour to his life?" Matthew 6:27 NIV

How often do you find yourself frustrated or worried by the circumstances around you? In my case it seems to be more often than not. The list of the sources for my frustration is long. Just a few that come to mind are children who just cannot get their lives together, employees who have trouble thinking past themselves, elderly relatives who are having health issues, social and civic demands on my life and countless other things that seem to be a part of everyday life. It would appear that most of my life is spent in frustration and worry. Does anyone else feel this way?

Today in my quiet time with God, His Word revealed to me that I am allowing things that I cannot change to frustrate me. If I know that I cannot change a situation, then why do I worry? I believe the answer is I want to be in control. If I am in control of all the things in my life, where is the need for God?

In some areas of my life, I do surrender all to God. Obviously, I need to be willing to turn everything else over to the Lord. The hard things are the personal issues. When it is personal, it is close to home. It affects me and the people around me.

God created the heavens and the earth and He is in complete control. The Bible tells us that not even a sparrow can fall to the ground without God knowing it. I do not worry whether the sun will rise tomorrow or if the seas will be in their places when I wake up. I am not concerned about having air to breathe or even food to eat. I know I have been given a home in Heaven. I know I have been saved by the grace of God and that Jesus Christ is my Savior. Why then do I worry and get frustrated about issues that pale in comparison? God is the Creator and He is in control, period.

Friend, if you are frustrated or worried by issues and circumstances you cannot seem to control, then get over it. Stop trying to be in control. Let God do what He wants to do. If He wants you to do something, He will tell you.

# Mother's Story

"And when men of that place recognized Jesus, they sent word to all the surrounding country. People brought all their sick to him and begged him to let the sick just touch the edge of his cloak, and all who touched him were healed." Matthew 14:35-36 NIV

I was visiting with my mother, and our conversation turned to how God provides and works in our lives, sometimes through the ordinary daily routines and, at other times, it is truly extraordinary. She relayed a story to me that I felt was worthy of repeating.

Several years ago, my mother began to lose the feeling in her legs as well as her mobility.

She gradually digressed from her usual fast-paced gait to more of a shuffle. Later, she was forced to go to a cane and then to a walker. The doctors she had been seeing had not been able to pinpoint the problem, and the family was becoming very concerned. Just before she was reduced to a wheel chair, new symptoms surfaced and specialists found that she had a very rare tumor on the lining of her spinal cord. This type of tumor is very slow-growing and, if not found and removed, will ultimately paralyze the person.

We were fortunate. Surgery was scheduled immediately. The tumor was removed successfully, and she was on her way to recovery. There was a problem though. Mother would be required to lie flat on her back and have little to no movement for a prolonged period of time.

As she lay in her bed at the hospital, she began to worry. She told herself, "I have been given a second chance to live a normal life. I am so afraid I am going to do something to mess this up." At that moment she felt a hand touch her shoulder. She turned her head to see who was in the room but no one was there. There was no other person in her room. She turned her head back and a feeling of peace flowed down from her head to her toes. She knew she had experienced a very special encounter with God. In her heart she knew everything was going to be just fine.

Some people have told her that she must have had an angel come and touch her. My mother thinks that it was God who touched her that day. I was not there, but I learned a long time ago that you do not argue with your mother. How wonderful is the touch of a Holy God. We all need to take more time to allow God to touch us in His very special way.

# Promises Not Kept

"The man of integrity walks securely, but he who takes crooked paths will be found out."
Proverbs 10:9 NIV

All of us have had promises made to us that have not been kept and, I dare say, all of us have made promises that we have not kept. These days it seems that it happens more often. Or maybe I just take notice of it more than I used to. Businessmen make promises that they cannot deliver on their products or on their ability to deliver them on time. It seems that you can say anything as long as you get the deal.

I was raised to believe that a man's word was his bond. Honest men did not need contracts. A handshake was good enough. In my younger days, I knew people who certainly fit that description. Unfortunately, that type of integrity does not appear to be the norm in our society today. Say what you want to in order to get the deal, but live up to only what is in the contract seems to be the banner of big business. "It is just business," they say.

Sadly, this mindset is also found outside of the business arena. Husbands fail to keep their word to their wives and wives do the same to their husbands. This is one of many reasons that the divorce rate continues to increase. Parents promise their children many things, but the delivery on them may be far and few between. Children promise their parents good grades and decent behavior, but the follow through may be lacking. The lack of integrity and honesty is killing the family.

Where does it all come from? Maybe it is because deep down inside many have lost the ability to recognize what is the truth and what is not. It could be that selfishness and a self-centered mindset have taken hold and what used to be important is no longer. Honesty and integrity are being placed on a dusty shelf and the world is paying a great price for it.

Where would we be if God the Father had decided not to make good on the promise to send Jesus to atone for our transgressions? Fortunately, God always keeps his promises. As Christians, we need to make sure that we keep our word and do exactly what we say we are going to do. If we cannot fulfill our promise, then we must be willing to admit it and ask for forgiveness and not make excuses. If we start now and then pass on a legacy of honesty and integrity, the world can and will change for the better. We can make a difference.

# A Part of Me

"Teach the older men to be temperate, worthy
of respect, self-controlled, and sound in faith,
in love and endurance." Titus 2:2 NIV

Yesterday, I spent time with an old and dear
friend. He is spending a few weeks in a skilled
nursing facility and hoping to return to his home.
His name is Wendell and he is 90 years old. He is
precious to me.

Wendell is one of those special individuals who
has the ability to do almost anything with his hands.
He has been a farmer, plumber, electrician, carpenter,
mechanic and many other practical things. Most
importantly, he is a lover of God and a true Christian
brother. For me, he has been an example of the older
man that today's verse talks about.

I grew up in a small rural community in Missouri.
We lived in town and Wendell and his family lived a
few miles out in the country. I was probably no more
than six or seven years old when Wendell stopped at
our home and asked my mother if he could take me

out to his farm and let me experience the harvesting of his wheat crop. That was the beginning of a long and wonderful friendship. The memories of those days will never leave my heart. A busy man took time to impart practical wisdom to a little boy and live an example that made a difference.

As time passed on we were always in touch. As a teenager I hunted rabbits on his farm. Later in life I took my son to hunt deer on that same farm. When I became a driver and we would pass each other on the road, we would wave or stop and speak. Wendell always had something good to say to me. I cannot remember a cross word in our conversations. I received nothing but encouragement and respect from him, and I returned nothing but the same.

Throughout my young adult life, Wendell continued to teach me practical and useful things so that home repairs and little projects became a source of joy rather than a bother. He was always eager to help me with a plumbing project or give me his opinion on how I might improve one of my building projects. He gave his opinion only when I asked for it. Isn't that unusual?

Even now, he still asks about my wife and children and shows a sincere concern for their well-being. He tells me that he is proud of what I have become and what I have done with my life. It is a wonderful thing to have someone who sees only the good in you and who does not remember the bad. It is one of those Godly qualities for which we should all strive. Wendell tells me that I need to keep pressing forward proclaiming God's Word. I think I will do just that. Wendell is a part of me. Will you be apart of another person's life?

# The Last Bus

"And I'll say to myself, 'You have plenty of good things laid up for many years. Take life easy; eat, drink and be merry.' But God said to him, 'You fool! This very night your life will be demanded from you. Then who will get what you have prepared for yourself?'"
Luke 12:19-20 NIV

A fellow once told me that he knew he needed to make a decision for Christ, but that he was waiting. He also informed me that he was sure he could always make a death bed confession. Does this work for you?

Deathbed confessions do happen I am sure. But, to place my hope in having that one last opportunity just does not work for me. How many times have we heard of an accident where the person was killed instantly? I have known people who were simply walking along feeling great and carrying on conversations with friends when suddenly they fell to the ground dead from a massive heart attack.

Life can be very short. Why someone would decide that he or she has plenty of time to accept Christ and secure eternity in Heaven is truly beyond me. I assume that for many it may be that they think they have to give up having fun and doing things that they like to do for a more religious life. Personally, I do not think that my life is boring and lacks fun. I do not consider myself to be a very religious person. I am a Christian and that means I have placed my faith in Jesus Christ. I do not get caught up in the do's and do not's of religion.

Maybe some people are afraid of changes that may occur in their life. The way I see it, God will only ask you to change what he wants you to change; if he asks you to do something, He will give you the will and the way to do it. If He gives you the desire to change, then it will not be a problem to make it. So what is the problem?

The person who is hoping that there will be time to repent and accept Christ as Savior just before their physical life ends, is playing with his spiritual eternity. It is like saying, "I am waiting till the last minute to buy the last ticket for the last seat on the last bus to Heaven." My question is, "What do you do if the bus leaves early?"

# Who am I to Judge?

"You judge by human standards: I pass judgment on no one." John 8:15 NIV.

These are the words of the one and only perfect man to walk the earth, Jesus Christ. I think many times we Christians fail to see that we view people and the world through flawed standards. The fact is we do primarily observe others and make judgments based on our own personal interpretation of spiritual and righteous living standards. Jesus preferred to not judge people at all.

The big difference isn't in judging. It is what or who you judge. Jesus had no problem pointing out sins or judging the actions of others, but He was able to do that without condemning the individual. You will find occasions in the Bible where the actions of people were condemned, but the individuals were not. Do you remember the woman caught in adultery? She was told to no longer sin, but our Lord did not judge or belittle her.

Have you ever in the heat of the moment caught yourself judging another? I dare say we all have. When a person is caught up in a sin they are truly a sinner. However, the problem is the action not the person. I have had people tell me that if they saw a Christian hanging around the local tavern, they would be forced to judge them. What if the person was picking up a friend or making an emergency phone call? I do not think Jesus would have rushed to judgment.

I know that I need to be very careful when a person commits an action that seems wrong on the surface. Do I have the whole story? I also need to ask myself if I am seeing things by human standards or by Gods. And, most importantly, am I judging the action or the person? If Jesus passed judgment on no one, then neither should I.

I have often heard it said, "Hate the sin, and love the sinner." In this case it could be easily said, "Judge the action, not the person."

# Weary and Tired

"He gives strength to the weary and increases the power of the weak. Even youths grow tired and weary, and young men stumble and fall; but those who hope in the Lord will renew their strength. They will soar on wings like eagles; they will run and not grow weary, they will walk and not be faint." Isaiah 40:29-31 NIV.

Does the weight of this world ever make you weary and tired? Of course it does. I confess that at this moment I am very weary and spiritually tired. And when I am spiritually stressed, I feel it physically. Likewise, when I am physically down, my spiritual reserves are taxed.

Let's look at some reasons why we may be weary and tired. How are we doing physically? Overweight, undernourished, not sleeping well, addictions, lack of exercise or just bad habits constantly tear us down physically. I am not completely unfit, but is there room to improve? That is a definite yes. If I lost 10 pounds, my knees would feel better. If my knees did not hurt, I would sleep better and if my sleep did not get interrupted, I would feel more like exercising. I think I see a pattern here. The big question is what am I going to do about it? The answer here is simple. I must take control of my health by eating right, exercising more and losing some weight.

Spiritually, how is your health? Relationship problems, worry, anger, distrust, lack of hope, an uncertain future, loneliness and the feeling of loss are just a few of the things that can ruin our spiritual health. What is the answer? Quite simply, let God take control, but you will need to do your part. Seek nourishment by reading your Bible on a consistent basis. Exercise your faith through prayer and possibly fasting. I suggest some serious deep knee bending before God. And finally, lose some weight. Let God have your burdens and worries. He is capable of taking care of them until He has renewed your strength so that they are not a burden for you at all.

So, what are we waiting for? Let's get healthy inside and out. We can soar! We can walk and run and not be weary or grow faint! What a deal!

# Perfectly New

"But our citizenship is in heaven. And we eagerly await a Savior from there, the Lord Jesus Christ, who, by the power that enables him to bring everything under his control, will transform our lowly bodies so that they will be like his glorious body." Philippians 3:20-21 NIV.

Today, I sit in the waiting room of the hospital awaiting the outcome of my mother's surgery. Mom is seventy-nine years old, and six months ago she had a perforated colon that required emergency surgery. At that time she was equipped with a temporary colostomy bag to allow her colon time to heal. It has been quite an ordeal for her and the family.

Today is a happy day for her because this surgery is to reattach her colon and eliminate the need for the temporary bypass. When everything is done she will no longer be tied to a device that restricts her mobility both physically and emotionally. Mobility is another word for freedom when it comes to my mom.

Her personal battle reminds me of a great promise we have from God. When our earthly bodies finally wear out and our time in this life has passed, we will receive new and glorious forms. They will be perfect in every aspect. They will not see disease or even age. The corruption that we call death will have no hold on these new bodies. Oh, what a wonderful thought! Most importantly, it is not just a thought but a promise. The Creator of the heavens will create new bodies for each of his children. Nothing of the old man and our fallen nature will remain, only perfection.

The doctor just came out to talk with us. The surgery went well. As he said, "No surprises." In only a few days, her colon should be functioning normally. When it comes to the new bodies that God has for us, when compared to eternity, it will only be a few days to perfection.

# Freedom

"Jesus replied, 'I tell you the truth, everyone who sins is a slave to sin. Now a slave has no permanent place in the family, but a son belongs to it forever. So if the Son sets you free, you will be free indeed.'" John 8:34-36 NIV

What is freedom? Today, our country celebrates its freedom as an independent nation. That freedom was bought with the blood of our ancestors. That same freedom has been protected by the blood of our citizens ever since. Maybe now, more than ever, I feel the sacrifice that so many families have made. My oldest son is now serving his country in the Army. Freedom is never given. It comes at a great cost.

Financial freedom requires hard work and the sacrifice of saving. Long hours may be required to get you there. Setting aside personal desires and dreams in order to save for the future good of the family can be hard and may seem impossible. Today's society does not promote such thinking. "Work less, play harder, get what you want now" is the banner being waved today. I have talked to many parents of grown children who seem to struggle financially. When you ask the parents what the problem might be, they almost always tell you the same thing. Their children want or expect now what it took them years to accomplish and accumulate.

Our spiritual freedom likewise came at a great cost. Our Savior, Jesus Christ, paid for it with his blood. He gave his life so that we would no longer be in bondage to our sinful nature. He came from Heaven with all its riches and majesty to live in the poverty and corruption created by the hands of mankind. He was hunted as a baby by an evil king who wanted to take his life. He lived his childhood in a poor community helping his adoptive father in a carpentry shop. Jesus later became a traveling evangelist without a home of his own. He worked long hours and yet many times had to rely on those around him to provide the finances for his ministry. Jesus was loved, revered, misunderstood and persecuted. Ultimately, He was betrayed, falsely accused and killed by those who did not understand his message or his mission. After He rose from the dead, they still refused to believe the truth.

We today owe our spiritual freedom to Jesus Christ. He was and is the one and only Son of the living God. It is a freedom that was bought with holy blood. Let us never forget.

# Peace

"I have told you these things, so that in me you may have peace. In this world you will have trouble. But take heart! I have overcome the world." John 16:33 NIV

Now more than ever I understand the peace that God can and will give us if we allow the Holy Spirit to lead us. Recently, my youngest son accompanied his grandfather on a fishing vacation in Mexico. What was supposed to be a wonderful vacation turned into something of a real nightmare for the family.

They left Monday morning early. At 11:00 pm our time we received news that our son had been in a serious ATV accident. The information was sketchy, to say the least. He had a broken leg and numerous cuts and bruises, but the severity was not known. My father is 78 years old and he was terribly upset that his 24 year-old grandson was hurt while in his care. He informed us that he would call back later to give us an update. My wife and I immediately prayed for everyone's safety and well being. Both of us felt a peace about the situation, and we knew that God would be in control, so we went to bed.

At 1:00 am Tuesday my father called back. Our son's leg was severely broken and so was his ankle. The hospital was also stitching up his face. Surgery was performed on his leg and a plate and 9 screws were inserted to immobilize the damaged bone. This was all being done in a hospital in Mexico, so there was always the question of quality of care in the back of our minds. But the peace remained. And we went back to sleep. I will be honest; it was not the best night's sleep that I have ever had, but, never the less, we were able to sleep.

Wednesday night at 11:00 pm we met the travelers at the airport. When we saw our son in a wheelchair and saw the damage to his body, especially the damage that was visible on his face, our hearts ached for him, but the peace that God had given us remained. It could have been worse. He was home alive and not in a box.

We learned that the hospital, although in Mexico, was owned and operated by an American company. His orthopedic surgeon was trained and certified in the United States. Our family physician tells us that he did a remarkable job in repairing a very severe injury. Obviously, God was in control and answering our prayers. The recovery will be long and the permanent damage and limitations are still unknown. Yet, peace still reigns in our hearts and in our home. We praise God for His mercy, grace and the gift of peace. Amen.

# Watch Your Mouth

"But now you must rid yourselves of all such things as these: anger, rage, malice, slander and filthy language from your lips."
Colossians 3:8 NIV

The words of a song from my childhood still ring in my ears today, "Oh, be careful little mouth what you say. Oh, be careful little mouth what you say. For the Father up above is looking down in love. Oh, be careful little mouth what you say." I would like to tell you that it has kept me from having unclean lips, but that is certainly not true. I can tell you that over the years I have improved, but it is still far too easy to slip back into sinful habits and say things that should have never been said.

The world around us has dulled the senses of many Christian people, including me. I have friends who are wonderful people, yet it is hard to be around them for an extended period of time. They have a tendency to make off-color jokes or sexual remarks that are offensive to the ears of those around them.

I am sure that I have been guilty of doing the same thing to others. This is the way of the old man. The new person in Christ does not have to take part in filthy language. Indeed, the Bible tells us to rid ourselves of such practices.

Today's media, radio, television, books and the movies do little to help you break such bad habits. They would like you to believe that it is the norm to be rude and crude with your speech. I challenge you to take the time to count the sexual and vulgar remarks in the next movie or television show you watch. You may be surprised that you have not noticed them before. The more we hear some things, the less we notice them. But, just because we do not notice, does not mean that we are not affected by them. The ultimate effect of hearing and ignoring filthy language is that it will infect your speech and your witness.

Our society is infected by all sorts of evil. Fortunately, we have the medicine that God has given to mankind to cure or rid us of these things. The cure is Jesus Christ. His Holy Spirit is here to remind us that we need to watch our mouths.

# Another Lesson Learned

"Keep my commands and you will live; guard my teachings as the apple of your eye. Bind them on your fingers; write them on the tablet of your heart." Proverbs 7:2-3 NIV

Sometimes the best stories are the ones that we can tell on ourselves. We have a great backyard with large trees and a branch. Occasionally a tree will die and I have to cut it down, leaving a stump. One such stump is the focus of my story.

A few years ago one of our neighbors was diagnosed with cancer. One of his daughters would come to our back yard with her niece and allow her to play with my grandchildren. While the children played, she would sit on a large stump of a dead elm tree. It was apparent that she was taking the time to contemplate life and how the family was going to deal with the inevitable loss of her father.

I was so touched by the scene I decided it would be a good thing to dedicate that stump as a place for quiet moments with God. I told my wife that I planned to carve a scripture verse into the side of the stump. I determined to use a portion of a verse from Psalms 46:10, "Be still, and know that I am God." I began to make my preparations.

One afternoon, I took my chainsaw and sliced off one side so that I could have a flat surface to carve. I then pulled out a set of wood chisels that I had purchased years ago but had never used. I penciled the verse on the stump and began to carve. It all sounds easy, doesn't it? Well, I soon found out that carving is an acquired talent, not a God- given gift. Two days later I was about half finished and becoming some- what agitated at my lack of ability.

I was in the process of gouging out the corner of a letter when the chisel slipped and struck the middle finger of my left hand. It hit right on the top joint. Immediately my hand closed in pain. All I could see was blood running from a clenched fist. My first thought was, "I have cut off the top of my finger." I took a deep breath and slowly opened my fist to take a look at the damage. The finger was still there, but the cut was very deep and would require stitches. Do you remember the scripture verse? I did not yell or panic. I gathered my tools, put them in my shop, and had my wife drive me to the emergency room for treatment. My grandsons were able to watch the doctor sew my finger back together.

Three weeks later I finished carving the stump, and it serves as a reminder that God is always there and ready to listen and give comfort, guidance and peace. I also know now why God wrote the Ten Commandments on stone instead of letting Moses do it.

# Compassion

"Therefore, as God's chosen people, holy and dearly loved, clothe yourselves with compassion, kindness, humility, gentleness and patience." Colossians 3:12 NIV

Do you really want to make a difference in the lives of others? Try showing compassion. This is an area where we all need improvement. Just in case you live in a vacuum and have not heard it, there are a lot of people out there who are hurting. The need for compassion is great.

As Christians we are God's chosen people. We are holy and dearly loved by God Himself. The verse for this study tells me that if I do not have or demonstrate compassion for others, then I am not fully clothed. In fact, I might be naked spiritually. Spiritual nakedness is not a very pleasant thought. It implies that we are lacking that outward appearance for which all Christians should strive, the appearance of Christ in our lives.

One never knows when the opportunity to be Christ to someone else will present itself. If we are compassionate to others, I guarantee there will be ample opportunities. I have a hard time believing that we can be truly compassionate without the other attributes that are mentioned. How can there be compassion that is not kind? What good is a compassion that is not humble? Do you really want to receive compassion with a harsh tone or attitude? And would anyone really appreciate compassion that was here today and gone tomorrow? Remember, patience is also known as long-suffering.

I will ask the question again, "Do you really want to make a difference in the lives of others?" If you know someone who has been hurt spiritually, lost a loved one, had a financial setback, has been diagnosed with a serious illness or maybe has never been introduced to Jesus Christ, then you have an opportunity to show compassion. Try it. The one receiving your compassion will appreciate it and you will receive a blessing by being clothed spiritually. Jesus showed us compassion. We can do the same.

# The Invitation

"Then the master told his servants, 'Go out to the roads and country lanes and make them come in, so that my house will be full.'" Luke 14:23 NIV

This verse is taken from the passage in the Bible that is known as The Parable of the Great Banquet. We know that this parable relates to God's invitation to mankind to accept His Son, Jesus Christ, as Lord and Savior, and then to enter into His presence. But I want to take us a little further into this setting to see another truth at work.

Let's not take anything away from the invitation, but we need to take a good look at who was supposed to deliver the invitation. The master told his servants to deliver his invitation to the people. I want to zero in on the servants. By doing so, I am going to be pointing a finger at you, as well as myself.

As Christians we are God's servants. We have been bought and paid for through the sacrifice made by Jesus Christ. We belong to God; He owns us. Call us servants or call us slaves; it really does not matter. Until the end of our time, we have a duty, and that is to go and take the Good News of Jesus Christ to a lost world, bringing in everyone who will accept the invitation. The verse says, "make them come in." The King James Version uses the word compel. In either case, it calls us to be strong and forceful. Whether you think you can be forceful with the invitation or not, it does not negate your orders.

Your orders do not necessarily ask you to give the plan of salvation to everyone you meet, but if you are able to do that, then by all means go for it. The orders do ask you to, in some way, be compelling enough that people want to know more. It can be as simple as asking them to attend worship services with you. Recently, I had a discussion with an acquaintance who was struggling with spiritual questions. I did not have all the answers, but I invited his family to come to church and participate in our Sunday morning Bible study. Believe it or not, they came. A few weeks later they brought a friend with them. Now, I am told that the friend has asked another person to start attending. My duty was to deliver the invitation and God did the rest. My prayer is that they will feast on His word, and they will invite others so that my Master's house will be full.

I have had people tell me that they did not feel adequate to do service for God. My answer for them is very simple. All you have to do is deliver the invitation.

# No Fear

"He replied, 'You of little faith, why are you so afraid?' Then he got up and rebuked the winds and the waves, and it was completely calm." Matthew 8:26 NIV

I have been told that there are 365 passages in the Bible that tell us no to be afraid. If God took the effort to tell us that many times not to fear or be afraid, then why do I still let fear take hold of my life?

What are we afraid of? I can give you quite a long list, but I will cut it short. Death, sickness, loss of loved ones, job security, war, poverty, politics, government, the economy and the list goes on. We also have smaller fears, such as the fear of failing that next test or losing our hair. We have fears that are not rational. People become paralyzed at the thought of flying or being in closed in places. Anyway we look at it, people seem to have a lot of things that make them afraid.

There is an answer to all our fears, and that is faith. How big is God? My God is bigger than anything that can come against me. His promises are greater than all the tragedy that the world can send me. God is more than able to overcome the problems of our world because He is the one who created all things.

Now, I want to set one thing straight so that there will be no confusion. God created all things and He created them to be good. Mankind, however, took what was good and corrupted it, and that is why so many things are evil or bad. These are the things that cause us to experience fear.

God never intended for us to live in fear. He wanted, and still wants us, to live in a faithful relationship with him. Adam and Eve had no fear until they became disobedient to God. Today, we still deal with fear because of our own disobedience. As a Christian, you might want to say to me, "I am not being disobedient." Romans 8:15 tells us this; "For you did not receive a spirit that makes you a slave again to fear, but you received the Spirit of sonship. And by him we cry, 'Abba, Father.'" If fear has control of your life, and you have not given it to the Father, then you might want to repent.

# Talk About High Anxiety

"Do not be anxious about anything, but in everything, by prayer and petition, with thanksgiving, present requests to God. And the peace of God, which transcends all understanding, will guard your hearts and your minds in Christ Jesus." Philippians 4:6-7 NIV.

Today has been one of those days that can cause a lot of anxiety. The economy is in a crisis. Wars are being waged on several fronts. The government appears dazed and confused. And then there are the personal issues that we all face.

A couple I know is facing personal issues that make the world's problems pale in comparison. They visited with me this morning and informed me that the husband has just been diagnosed with colon cancer. He is anticipating undergoing surgery soon. His mother is already dying of cancer and is not expected to live to the end of the year. They informed me that he must travel 40 miles one way to see his cancer specialist and that their car is not truly road worthy and cannot be trusted to make the trip. On top of that, they have limited resources since both of them must survive on social security disability.

This is a Christian couple who are now dealing with the effects of their past before they met Christ. To say they are anxious is an understatement. I could not sit on the other side of my desk and tell them that they had to have faith and that everything would work out. They need a car and they need one now. My wife and I have prayed about the matter and have decided to find a car that will suit their needs and purchase it for them. They do not know what we are planning to do, and I have no intention of telling them it came from us.

My hope for them is that they will become less anxious about things when this particular need is met. Anxiety will only compound the effects of an illness. I am convinced that as they pray and make their requests to the Heavenly Father, and they are met in very special ways through others who serve God, that the anxiety levels will continue to diminish.

He told me, "I know that if I die, I will go to Heaven, but I worry about my family." My response to him was, "First of all, friend, you aren't dead yet, and God is big enough to take care of you and your family." High anxiety has a cure and it is God.

# Provision

"As for God, his way is perfect: the word of the Lord is flawless. He is a shield for all who take refuge in him." 2 Samuel 22:31 NIV

God is always amazing. In the last lesson, I told you about a couple going through hard times who needed a car in the worst way. I am not surprised to tell you that God came through in a way that I did not see or expect.

Since my wife and I came to an agreement that God wanted us to help this couple, we took on the task of finding a dependable car for a reasonable price. After talking to many dealers, I found that what I considered dependable and reasonably priced was not the same as other people thought. It did not take long for me to get frustrated. God's small, still voice spoke to me and told me to relax and take it to our church congregation for their consideration.

Sunday morning, I let our Bible study class know the situation and asked them to be on the lookout for a good car. One of the men in the study said he might have an answer and to see him after class. I caught up with him just before worship service and he let me know that he had a car that he wanted to give away. It needed tires and a little brake work, but other than that, it was in good shape. I eagerly accepted his offer and made arrangements to pick it up and get the repairs completed. Within two days, the car was in the hands of new and very grateful owners.

The lesson I have learned from this is very simple. Just because God tells you to do something, it doesn't mean you have to plan everything. I spent several days looking for a car that only God knew where it was. God knew my heart was right and wanted me to work with his plan, not make my own plan to serve him. The plans of men are imperfect, but when God makes the plan, it is perfectly amazing. Once again I stand amazed at the provision of the Heavenly Father.

# Appearances: The Sow's Ear

"Stop judging by mere appearances, and make a right judgment." John 7:24 NIV

Aren't you glad that God does not judge us by our appearance? Every since I can remember, I have heard the saying, "You can not make a silk purse out of a sow's ear." Most of the time, it was used in a derogatory sense. People were indicating that someone of lesser means was unable to rise above their circumstances. I have never been able to believe that this is true.

I have a true story involving the sow's ear that gives an illustration that not everything is as it seems. I know a man who has created a business based on sows' ears. Yes, that is right, sows' ears. I met Joe several years ago at a golf tournament. He was a very happy fellow because he had just received a truckload of sows' ears. Being by nature curious I had to know how a truck full of animal ears could be a good thing, so I asked him about sows' ears. To my surprise, I found out that a sow's ear, properly processed and packaged, is sold at pet stores all over the country as a gourmet chew treat for dogs.

I knew that sows, (female pigs for the city people who are reading this) after they are no longer useful in producing young pigs, are sent to processing centers to be used in food productions. I had not thought about where such by-products as ears went. Joe may not be making silk purses, but at the end of the day, he certainly can buy one for his wife. What many would consider worthless has become the source of a thriving business.

If God judged us by our outward appearance, how would we shape up? I know that I am not a silk purse for certain. In some people's eyes I might be considered a sow's ear. Whether I am a silk purse or a sow's ear is not of concern to me because I know that God loves me and has a use for me in his kingdom plan. And if the God of Creation has a use for me, then He has a use for those whom I might consider to be of lesser means. Forgive me Lord when I judge by the outward appearance of another. Amen.

# Retirement

"And I'll say to myself, 'You have plenty of good things stored up for many years. Take life easy; eat, drink and be merry.'" Luke 12:19 NIV

This verse seems to fit the description or expectation of many people who plan to retire. The truth is, the verse is just a portion of a larger passage. The next verse tells us how the man was not going to be able to enjoy what he had stored up because God knew that his life would be lost that very night. Life is uncertain and so is what we call retirement.

I have searched the Bible trying to find a passage that sanctions retirement, but I have not succeeded. I have found many verses that tell us of the virtues of work and of the consequences of not working. Retirement, however, does not appear to be a right or a necessity in the Scriptures. Does this sound like bad news to you? I ask you to consider something. Look around and you will find many people who have retired from their work. Some are very happy and some are worried and troubled. What do you think the difference is?

The happy person is usually still very busy doing some sort of work. They are plugged in to their church and the needs of the body. They are active in the community and work around their homes. They are participating in the personal lives of their families and friends. They have a purpose. They are still at work.

Those who are worried and troubled have pulled away from church, family and friends and become concerned about possessions and wealth. They do not get out and meet with people. Physical strength is lost due to inactivity. And then to make it worse, the Bible tells us that idle people, because they are not busy, become busybodies. I can understand the worry, especially in trying economic times. Pension funds and retirement plans that are tied to mutual funds and the stock market can take a beating. Plans one might have made may need to go on hold. If we are not active and busy in some kind of work, we have too much time to consider our plight.

I believe that God wants us all to keep working for the Kingdom. We may not need to keep that nine-to-five job, but we must stay busy and work because we do not know when the Master will return. From Gods' work there is no retirement.

# Elections and the Elect

"Everyone must submit himself to the governing authorities, for there is no authority except that which God has established. The authorities that exist have been established by God." Romans 13:1 NIV

Our historic election is now over. Whether your candidate won or lost, and how you deal with it, is left up to you. The one thing that everyone is in agreement with, is it is finally over. Most people I know are worn out by all the media coverage and the negativity that was associated with this election. Regardless of whom you voted for, you have an obligation under God to pray for the leaders of our country. Is that bad news for you? I will let the Holy Spirit and you work that out.

Now, here is the issue that really got me going during the election. Many of my Christian friends were very vocal about their politics. Some are Democrats and some are Republicans. Their political affiliation is not my concern. What does concern me is that they were very outspoken on candidates and issues during the election, but they never spoke of Christ. Why is it that we can become passionate about politics, but show no passion about the most important person in our life?

Has God become so unimportant to us that we have forgotten how to praise Him? I pray that this is not the case. Does God's salvation no longer stir our hearts so that we do not think to share the good news? Heaven forbid that this could be true. What a difference we could make in this country and the world if our passion for God was displayed with the enthusiasm given to politics. It makes you wonder if the Christian community has bought into the idea of separation of church and state. While I agree that no denomination should be in control of our government, I also believe that our government would be better off if it were God centered.

Maybe people, even some Christians, find politics more interesting than the God of Creation. I again pray that this is not true. If there is truth in this thought, then I pray that collectively, we Christians repent and pray for a revival to fall upon our land. Lives need to be changed, and if our priorities are not in proper alignment, we are in for hard times. I simply believe that if God is first in my life, then I need to act like it.

# Old Friends

"They asked each other, 'Were not our hearts
burning within us while he talked with us on
the road and opened the Scriptures to us?'"
Luke 24:32 NIV

I visited with a couple today who had moved away
from the area and our church many years ago.
When I first saw them today, I had no problem recog-
nizing their faces. As soon as we started talking, my
memory was flooded with past experiences with
them. The bond of Christianity is truly a wonderful
asset to a friendship. Even though we had been separated over the years, our love for one another was
still very evident.

It started with all the usual pleasantries but
became personal very quickly. How are the children
and grandchildren? What about health issues? How
are other people at the church? Is the church growing?
How are you doing in your ministries? There were so
many questions and we had so little time. I longed
to be able to spend the day with them; but, unfortu-

nately, schedules did not allow for that. Even though the visit was short, our time together was priceless.

All of us have some good Christian friends for whom we have not taken the time for recent visits. What a mistake this is! When we have like thinking from kindred hearts, we are strengthened as we visit. In fact, many times when we visit with our Christian friends, we find that our hearts burn with excitement when we discuss our Savior and what He has done for us? I think that is because even though we are talking to friends, our best friend is right there with us interacting through the Holy Spirit.

Now, let us take this thought a step further. How is your friendship with God? Is it as close as it should be? When you pray, does your heart burn? When you read the Gospel, do you feel the friendship or do you fall asleep? If you do not have that burning heart or if the Scriptures do not excite you, then you might want to take a reality check on your friendship with God. Has friendship with the world taken over your heart? If so, repent and seek out your first love. He is waiting to rekindle the fire that we all need and should want.

# Tell Me, Why?

> "I tell you that anyone who divorces his wife, except for marital unfaithfulness, and marries another woman commits adultery." Matthew 19:9 NIV

This is a time when I feel compelled to write about something that may offend some of my readers. It is not my intention to hurt or offend anyone, but the issue of divorce is destroying our families and the moral fabric of our country. Every time you turn around someone is talking about or getting a divorce. What is going on!

In this last year numerous men and women I know, who claim to be Christians, have either separated from or divorced their spouse. The reasons or excuses vary from case to case, but most of them do not come under the reason that Jesus gave. I hear things like, "We just do not love each other the way we used to," or "I feel trapped." Another excuse is, "I just do not want to be married anymore." These excuses are shallow and controlled by emotion, not by God's commands.

Being a minister, I get great enjoyment from performing wedding ceremonies, but I am saddened by the fact that possibly fifty percent of those couples will someday end up before a judge who will terminate what God had initiated. In some cases it may only be a few years. Unfortunately, today, we are seeing couples divorce after many years of marriage. I know of at least three recently that involve over twenty years of marriage in each case. How do you throw away twenty years of life and relationship?

The Bible tells us that God hates divorce. Why do you think that is? Personally, I believe it is because of the broken relationships. With divorce it is not just the couple who feel the effects. Children, parents, family and friends are all damaged by the process. Confusion reigns when divorce happens. People blame themselves or others. Children think it is their fault that mom and dad cannot live together. Friends feel compelled to choose sides. Little is gained and plenty is lost. What a mess!

Now, I do understand that there are reasons for divorce. A spouse is expected to remain faithful in the marriage contract. No one should be physically or emotionally abused. Other reasons can be listed, but they fall under the category of unfaithfulness. It is unfaithfulness to God that has allowed humanity to fall to such moral decay that love and marriage have lost their meaning. May God helps us to love and care more about our spouse and family than our personal selfish desires.

# Thanksgiving More than a Day Off

"Be joyful always; pray continually; give thanks in all circumstances, for this is God's will for you in Christ Jesus." 1 Thessalonians 5:16-18 NIV

As I write this lesson I am still trying to come up with a plan to burn off the calories I gained from the Thanksgiving holiday. I am sure that I am not alone. Thanksgiving, what a holiday! Take family, friends, fellowship and lots of food, mix them together and there you have it-Thanksgiving. By the end of the day most of us are tired, weary, and beat.

True, thanksgiving is more than just a holiday. It is an attitude that God tells us we need to have working at all times. How do you do that in a world that is broken by sin? After all, does anyone really expect me to be joyful, prayerful and thankful when things are going bad? When the economy is awful and jobs are scarce, am I supposed to be joyful?

When my children or other family members do not seem to appreciate me, am I expected to be thankful? When my health is not good or things are not going well at home or at work, it is easy to become more prayerful. Unfortunately, when things get better, my private prayer times may become shorter and the thanksgiving is often very brief.

Most of us have a hard time seeing the good in bad situations. But if you look hard enough and seek God's wisdom you might be able to surprise yourself. Where am I going with this? Well, the economy is bad and I am worried about my job, but I still have a job and for that I am thankful. I can pray that things will turn around and be joyful in the fact that God is in ultimate control of this world and not man. Things may be bad, but I have food, shelter, clothing, family and friends.

Someday, I may get sick. For now, I am thankful that I have my health, but if a time comes that I do not, I can take joy in the fact that God has given wisdom to doctors and other people in the health care industry for my care. We can give thanks that every day cures for diseases have been found. What used to be deadly can now be treated, and we can pray that other cures will be found. Most importantly, I know that even if illness takes my life, it is not over. It is then that I will see my Savior face to face and my joy will be complete. For this I am joyful, prayerful and very thankful.

# Romance

"'Well done, my good servant!' his master replied. 'Because you have been trustworthy in a very small matter, take charge of ten cities.'" Luke 19:17 NIV

Romance is not what Hollywood or other popular medias portray it to be. In fact, it is very much the opposite. It is not about the moment, but it is about time. It is not about the event, but it is about the planning that leads up to it. Romance is not truly found in the passion, but passion's source flows from patience. True romance involves desire and faithfulness. A desire to be faithful in the small details of a relationship is essential to romance.

My wife and I have been married thirty-five years and we dated for two years before that. I can tell you that we still hold hands when we walk together, whether it is a quiet stroll in the woods or in the local shopping mall. I still open doors for her; yes, even car doors upon occasion. It is the little things we do for each other that prove we still care.

I have watched people all my life, paying special attention to couples and how they interact. I am amazed by some and amused by others. There are also those couples who leave you absolutely confused. I remember well the couple who celebrated their seventy-sixth wedding anniversary in the nursing home. He was ninety-seven and she was one hundred and one. The love and respect of their relationship was a wonderful example to all who were present. Then there was the young couple who returned from their honeymoon and immediately filed for divorce. Obviously, the passion and the moment were not up to their expectations or enough to secure the relationship.

God's Word tells us to be faithful or trustworthy in the little matters, and greater rewards and responsibility will follow. Paying attention to the small details of your marriage relationship will increase the reward of romance, not as the world knows it, but as God intended it. If a couple will be trustworthy in the small details of their life with each other, they will be rewarded with love, faithfulness, friendship, passion and intimacy. All these and more are the final products of romance.

# Celebrating Christmas

"But you, Bethlehem, in the land of Judah, are by no means least among the rulers of Judah; for out of you will come a ruler who will be the shepherd of my people Israel." Matthew 2:6 NIV

"But the angel said to them, 'Do not be afraid. I bring you good news of great joy that will be for all the people. Today in the town of David a Savior has been born to you; he is Christ the Lord.'" Luke 2:10-11 NIV

Sitting at my desk today, I caught myself doing something that I need to be doing more often. In my mind and in my heart I was singing Christmas carols. To be exact it was, "O Little Town of Bethlehem". It is a good thing that I was not singing out loud because I see no reason to scare any children who might pass by.

Why is it so easy to get caught up in the true spirit of Christmas? For me the answer is simple. This is the time of year that Christians corporately celebrate the birth of my Lord and Savior, Jesus Christ. It is to Jesus that my heart sings. I joyfully celebrate this time because I have been set free from the bondage of sin and death. What a wonderful gift to receive.

Jesus is the greatest gift ever given to mankind. Nothing can or ever will compare to God sending his Son to a lost and dying world. But, I wonder why I do not sing songs of praise and honor in my heart more often? Do I really need a holiday season to remind me of the ultimate goodness sent my way? I do often find myself praising God, but I am sure I can do much better. Every breath that I take is one more than I deserve. Every moment that passes is one closer to Heaven.

How well do you celebrate the birth of the Savior? Hopefully, it is more than just during the Christmas or Easter holidays. Times may be difficult and life uncertain, but God has seen fit to show compassion to all who will receive it. Grace has been given to us. May we sing always, even if it is only in our hearts, of God's greatest gift, Jesus Christ.

# Remember

"No longer will a man teach his neighbor or a man his brother, saying 'Know the Lord,' because they will know me, from the least to the greatest," declares the Lord. "For I will forgive their wickedness and will remember their sins no more." Jeremiah 31:34 NIV

While at a Christmas function the other day and I was talking to an old friend with whom I went to high school. Immediately, my mind took me to a situation that at the time was not pleasant. As I look back on it now, it is quite funny and was the result of my own stupidity. We both survived the episode and are able to laugh about it.

What do you remember about people when you see or think about them? Are they good memories or are they bad? Do they make you happy or do they bring you sadness or hurt? If they do not make you feel good about the person or yourself, then you need to discard the thoughts and forgive the person or yourself. We need to follow God's example. The

Bible tells us that when God forgives us He remembers it no more.

When I conduct a funeral service I like to tell the family who has lost a loved one that they should dwell on the good memories about the person and refuse to think anything bad about the relationship. I know what I am saying may be difficult, if not impossible, in today's world. Sin has so corrupted our relationships, that some may have absolutely nothing positive to remember. This is sad indeed. As a general rule, however, most relationships have both good and bad mixed in, just like our relationship with God.

Mankind wants to keep a record of the bad memories and allow them to overshadow the good. God keeps record of our good and rejoices in it. He does not ever return to what he has forgiven. To revisit our sins would nullify the work of God's Son, Jesus Christ. He gave his life so that all who believe may be saved from their sins. His death on the cross is why the Heavenly Father is willing to forgive and forget the bad that we do. God does not have amnesia. It is a willful forgetfulness and one that we should all try to emulate.

May God grant all his children the ability to forgive and forget and may we keep the good memories alive.

Printed in the United States
211761BV00001B/3/P

9 781607 913894